"The traffic stop"

The only thing routine is the hunt!

All rights reserved. No part of this publication may be reproduced, distributed, or transmitted in any form or by any means, including photocopying, recording, or other electronic or mechanical methods, without the prior written permission of the publisher, except in the case of brief quotations embodied in critical reviews and certain other noncommercial uses permitted by copyright law.

DISCLAIMER

This book is a resource and all content should be used as such. This doesn't supersede local, state, and/or federal law. This book also doesn't supersede your department policy. The views expressed in this book are those of the author(s) and don't represent the views of any company or agency they work with or for.

The traffic stop

The traffic stop is our bread and butter in law enforcement next to a subject stop. It separates the hard chargers from the lot lizards in our profession. When done safely and within the legal restrictions given to us, it can produce fruits beyond your imagination and hours of entertainment.

While some jurisdictions are cutting down traffic violations and moving key violations to secondary violations, your skillset must evolve and adapt to newer strategies to do what you took an oath to, protect the public.

Let's address the growing number of District Attorneys and Commonwealth Attorneys who are placating a very small group of people and creating potentially a very dangerous environment for law-abiding citizens. The "De-criminalizing" term drives me absolutely insane. Just call it what it is, you don't support the infraction or law so instead of doing what's right by having the people vote to eliminate it you've sidestepped the process. It's a public relations word game to appease a small base of voters while the other half stays quiet till crime rates skyrocket.

These same traffic violations or moving violations are the same ones that aided in the arrest of serial killers and terrorists. How? Ted Bundy who admitted to killing multiple women was apprehended from a traffic stop. A beat cop who was out doing his job and pushing a sector car spotted old Ted roll through a stop sign. He didn't brush it off or turn the other way.

On April 19, 1995, Oklahoma State Trooper Charles J. Hanger spotted a yellow 1997 Mercury Marquies driving on interstate 35 in Noble County. Trooper Hanger observed the vehicle with no license plate. During the traffic stop, Trooper Hanger noticed a bulge under the jacket of the driver. During questioning the driver admitted to having a concealed weapon and was subsequently arrested for possessing an illegal weapon and driving without plates. That driver was Timmothy McVeigh and he had just left carrying out one of the largest terrorist attacks on United States soil. From a "simple" traffic stop. In

1995, technology was not as advanced as today, intel not as readily available, and training not as advanced as today, but Trooper Hanger used his core training, experience, and intuition to catch one of the most violent terrorists in history. FROM A TRAFFIC STOP!

On August 10, 1977 officers from the Yonkers Police Department (New York) approached a parked yellow Ford Galaxie. This vehicle was flagged by the NYPD in a homicide investigation. The driver was a person of interest in several homicides. The Yonkers officers approached the vehicle and observed a handgun in the back seat in plain view. The officers conducted a search of the parked car and located a duffle bag containing maps of the crime scenes, ammunition, and a threatening letter to NYPD Inspector Timothy Dowd of the Omega Task Force. Officers decided to wait for the owner of the vehicle to exit his apartment and get into the vehicle to limit the risk to the public and officers. When the owner exited his apartment and got into his vehicle a traffic stop was conducted and David Berkowitz was arrested. David Berkowitz, "The son of Sam" admitted to eight shootings in New York City and later plead guilty to killing six and wounding nine. He was sentenced to six life sentences.

These examples of traffic stops are for you to understand that it doesn't take a fancy radar unit or the latest thermal technology to score a big fish. You need skills that come over time and some of the things discussed by Dave, Mike, and me in this book. Asking the same questions on every traffic stop and permission to search a vehicle from a soccer mom to a gang banger is not a waste of time, it's zeroing your skill.

In your traffic stop script, what are you asking? What are you requesting consent on? What do your searches look like? Are you getting rejected a majority of the time when you ask for consent to search? Are you adjusting your style to gain compliance?

These are valid questions that you should ask yourself on a routine basis. If you're not doing this, start. Partner with veterans or Facebook groups and get advice on how they structure questions during traffic stops. You'd be amazed at how changing a slight word or phrase can gain compliance and permission. Every person provides you with a different perspective and possibly a new skill.

More than anything your department policy, city, county, and state laws must be adhered to and in no way are Mike, Dave, or I telling you to do anything outside the scope of that.

Case law

Case law is our bread and butter. It's what any good cop understands thoroughly and can articulate exceptionally. When I speak about case law I'm referring to the big ones that should be ingrained in our brains. Where some of our comrades get into the "grey zone" is cherry-picking obscure cases that slant view to match what you're trying to achieve. If you currently do that, STOP. If you need to find loopholes or your own interpretations of case law, you're doing it all wrong and you will get a reputation among judges and defense attorneys.

Here are a few case laws that not only deal with traffic stops but search and seizure and other benefits to know.

Terry v. Ohio, 392 U.S. 1 (1968)

Terry v. Ohio

No. 67

Argued December 12, 1967

Decided June 10, 1968

392 U.S. 1[1]

Syllabus

A Cleveland detective (McFadden), on a downtown beat which he had been patrolling for many years, observed two strangers (petitioner and another man, Chilton) on a street corner. He saw them proceed alternately back and forth along an identical route, pausing to stare in the same store window, which they did for a total of

---

[1] https://supreme.justia.com/cases/federal/us/392/1/

about 24 times. Each completion of the route was followed by a conference between the two on a corner, at one of which they were joined by a third man (Katz) who left swiftly. Suspecting the two men of "casing a job, a stick-up," the officer followed them and saw them rejoin the third man a couple of blocks away in front of a store. The officer approached the three, identified himself as a policeman, and asked their names. The men "mumbled something," whereupon McFadden spun petitioner around, patted down his outside clothing, and found in his overcoat pocket, but was unable to remove, a pistol. The officer ordered the three into the store. He removed petitioner's overcoat, took out a revolver, and ordered the three to face the wall with their hands raised. He patted down the outer clothing of Chilton and Katz and seized a revolver from Chilton's outside overcoat pocket. He did not put his hands under the outer garments of Katz (since he discovered nothing in his pat-down which might have been a weapon), or under petitioner's or Chilton's outer garments until he felt the guns. The three were taken to the police station. Petitioner and Chilton were charged with carrying concealed weapons. The defense moved to suppress the weapons. Though the trial court rejected the prosecution theory that the guns had been seized during a search incident to a lawful arrest, the court denied the motion to suppress and admitted the weapons into evidence on the ground that the officer had cause to believe that petitioner and Chilton were acting suspiciously, that their interrogation was warranted, and that the officer, for his own protection, had the right to pat down their outer clothing having reasonable cause to believe that they might be armed. The court distinguished between an investigatory "stop" and an arrest, and between a "frisk" of the outer clothing for weapons and a full-blown search for evidence of crime. Petitioner and Chilton were found guilty, an intermediate appellate court affirmed, and the State Supreme Court dismissed the appeal on the ground that "no substantial constitutional question" was involved.

Held:

1. The Fourth Amendment right against unreasonable searches and seizures, made applicable to the States by the Fourteenth Amendment, "protects people, not places," and therefore applies as much to the citizen on the streets as well as at home or elsewhere. Pp. 392 U. S. 8-9.

2. The issue in this case is not the abstract propriety of the police conduct, but the admissibility against petitioner of the evidence uncovered by the search and seizure. P. 392 U. S. 12.

3. The exclusionary rule cannot properly be invoked to exclude the products of legitimate and restrained police investigative techniques, and this Court's approval of such techniques should

not discourage remedies other than the exclusionary rule to curtail police abuses for which that is not an effective sanction. Pp. 392 U.S. 13-15.

4. The Fourth Amendment applies to "stop and frisk" procedures such as those followed here. Pp. 392 U. S. 16-20.

(a) Whenever a police officer accosts an individual and restrains his freedom to walk away, he has "seized" that person within the meaning of the Fourth Amendment. P. 392 U. S. 16.

(b) A careful exploration of the outer surfaces of a person's clothing in an attempt to find weapons is a "search" under that Amendment. P. 392 U. S. 16.

5. Where a reasonably prudent officer is warranted in the circumstances of a given case in believing that his safety or that of others is endangered, he may make a reasonable search for weapons of the person believed by him to be armed and dangerous

Page 392 U. S. 3

regardless of whether he has probable cause to arrest that individual for crime or the absolute certainty that the individual is armed. Pp. 392 U. S. 20-27.

(a) Though the police must, whenever practicable, secure a warrant to make a search and seizure, that procedure cannot be followed where swift action based upon on-the-spot observations of the officer on the beat is required. P. 392 U. S. 20.

(b) The reasonableness of any particular search and seizure must be assessed in light of the particular circumstances against the standard of whether a man of reasonable caution is warranted in believing that the action taken was appropriate. Pp. 392 U. S. 21-22.

(c) The officer here was performing a legitimate function of investigating suspicious conduct when he decided to approach petitioner and his companions. P. 392 U. S. 22.

(d) An officer justified in believing that an individual whose suspicious behavior he is investigating at close range is armed may, to neutralize the threat of physical harm, take necessary measures to determine whether that person is carrying a weapon. P. 392 U. S. 24.

(e) A search for weapons in the absence of probable cause to arrest must be strictly circumscribed by the exigencies of the situation. Pp. 392 U. S. 25-26.

(f) An officer may make an intrusion short of arrest where he has reasonable apprehension of danger before being possessed of information justifying arrest. Pp. 392 U. S. 26-27.

6. The officer's protective seizure of petitioner and his companions and the limited search which he made were reasonable, both at their inception and as conducted. Pp. 392 U. S. 27-30.

(a) The actions of petitioner and his companions were consistent with the officer's hypothesis that they were contemplating a daylight robbery and were armed. P. 392 U. S. 28.

(b) The officer's search was confined to what was minimally necessary to determine whether the men were armed, and the intrusion, which was made for the sole purpose of protecting himself and others nearby, was confined to ascertaining the presence of weapons. Pp. 392 U. S. 29-30.

7. The revolver seized from petitioner was properly admitted into evidence against him, since the search which led to its seizure was reasonable under the Fourth Amendment. Pp. 392 U. S. 30-31.

Affirmed.

Page 392 U. S. 4

Pennsylvania v. Mimms, 434 U.S. 106 (1977)

Pennsylvania v. Mimms

No. 76-1830

Decided December 5, 1977

434 U.S. 106

Syllabus

After police officers had stopped respondent's automobile for being operated with an expired license plate, one of the officers asked respondent to step out of the car and produce his license and registration. As respondent alighted, a large bulge under his jacket was noticed by the officer, who thereupon frisked him and found a loaded revolver. Respondent was then arrested and subsequently indicted for carrying a concealed weapon and unlicensed firearm. His motion to suppress the revolver was denied and after a trial, at which the revolver was introduced in evidence, he was convicted. The Pennsylvania

---

[2] https://supreme.justia.com/cases/federal/us/434/106/

Supreme Court reversed on the ground that the revolver was seized in violation of the Fourth Amendment.

Held:

1. The order to get out of the car, issued after the respondent was lawfully detained, was reasonable, and thus permissible under the Fourth Amendment. The State's proffered justification for such order -- the officer's safety -- is both legitimate and weighty, and the intrusion into respondent's personal liberty occasioned by the order, being, at most, a mere inconvenience, cannot prevail when balanced against legitimate concerns for the officer's safety.

2. Under the standard announced in *Terry v. Ohio,* 392 U. S. 1, 392 U. S. 21-22 -- whether

"the facts available to the officer at the moment of the seizure or the search 'warrant a man of reasonable caution in the belief that the action taken was appropriate"
-- the officer was justified in making the search he did once the bulge in the respondent's jacket was observed.

Certiorari granted; 471 Pa. 546, 370 A.2d 1157, reversed and remanded.

Kansas v. Glover was a case argued before the Supreme Court of the United States on November 4, 2019, during the court's October 2019-2020

---

[3] https://ballotpedia.org/Kansas_v._Glover

term. The case came on a *writ* of *certiorari* to the Kansas Supreme Court.

The court reversed and remanded the decision of the Kansas Supreme Court in an 8-1 ruling, holding that when an officer lacks information negating an inference that the vehicle's owner is driving the vehicle, an investigative traffic stop made after running a vehicle's license plate and learning that the registered owner's driver's license has been revoked is reasonable under the Fourth Amendment.[1] Click here for more information.

HIGHLIGHTS

The case: A Douglas County police officer stopped Charles Glover on suspicion of driving without a valid license. The officer did not witness any traffic violations. Glover was charged with driving as a habitual violator. Glover moved to suppress evidence from the stop, arguing the officer violated Glover's Fourth Amendment rights. The state district court agreed, dismissing the case. On appeal, the Kansas Court of Appeals reversed the district court's ruling. Glover petitioned the Kansas Supreme Court for review. The state supreme court affirmed the district court's ruling, dismissing the case.

The issue: Whether, for purposes of an investigative stop under the Fourth Amendment, it is reasonable for an officer to suspect that the registered owner of a vehicle is the one driving the vehicle absent any information to the contrary.

The outcome: The court reversed and remanded the Kansas Supreme Court's decision in an 8-1 ruling, holding that when an officer lacks information negating an inference that the vehicle's owner is driving the vehicle, an investigative traffic stop made after running a vehicle's license plate and learning that the registered owner's driver's license has been revoked is reasonable under the Fourth Amendment.[1]

WHREN ET AL. *v.* UNITED STATES

CERTIORARI TO THE UNITED STATES COURT OF APPEALS FOR THE DISTRICT OF COLUMBIA CIRCUIT

No. 95-5841. Argued April 17, 1996-Decided June 10, 1996[4]

Plainclothes policemen patrolling a "high drug area" in an unmarked vehicle observed a truck driven by petitioner Brown waiting at a stop sign at an intersection for an unusually long time; the truck then turned suddenly, without signaling, and sped off at an "unreasonable" speed. The officers stopped the vehicle, assertedly to warn the driver about traffic violations, and upon approaching the truck observed plastic bags of crack cocaine in petitioner Whren's hands. Petitioners were arrested. Prior to trial on federal drug charges, they moved for suppression of the evidence, arguing that the stop had not been justified by

---

[4] https://supreme.justia.com/cases/federal/us/517/806/

either a reasonable suspicion or probable cause to believe petitioners were engaged in illegal drug-dealing activity, and that the officers' traffic-violation ground for approaching the truck was pretextual. The motion to suppress was denied, petitioners were convicted, and the Court of Appeals affirmed.

Held: The temporary detention of a motorist upon probable cause to believe that he has violated the traffic laws does not violate the Fourth Amendment's prohibition against unreasonable seizures, even if a reasonable officer would not have stopped the motorist absent some additional law enforcement objective. Pp. 809-819.

(a) Detention of a motorist is reasonable where probable cause exists to believe that a traffic violation has occurred. See, *e. g., Delaware* v. *Prouse,* 440 U. S. 648, 659. Petitioners claim that, because the police may be tempted to use commonly occurring traffic violations as means of investigating violations of other laws, the Fourth Amendment test for traffic stops should be whether a reasonable officer would have stopped the car for the purpose of enforcing the traffic violation at issue. However, this Court's cases foreclose the argument that ulterior motives can invalidate police conduct justified on the basis of probable cause. See, *e. g., United States* v. *Robinson,* 414 U. S. 218, 221, n. 1, 236. Subjective intentions play no role in ordinary, probable-cause Fourth Amendment analysis. Pp. 809-813.

(b) Although framed as an empirical question-whether the officer's conduct deviated materially from standard police practices-petitioners' proposed test is plainly designed to combat the perceived danger of pretextual stops. It is thus inconsistent with this Court's cases, which make clear that the Fourth Amendment's concern with "reasonableness" allows certain actions to be taken in certain circumstances, *whatever* the subjective intent. See, *e. g., Robinson, supra,* at 236. Nor can the Fourth Amendment's protections be thought to vary from place to place and from time to time, which would be the consequence of assessing the reasonableness of police conduct in light of local law enforcement practices. Pp. 813-816.

(c) Also rejected is petitioners' argument that the balancing of interests inherent in Fourth Amendment inquiries does not support enforcement of minor traffic laws by plainclothes police in unmarked vehicles, since that practice only minimally advances the government's interest in traffic safety while subjecting motorists to inconvenience, confusion, and anxiety. Where probable cause exists, this Court has found it necessary to engage in balancing only in cases involving searches or seizures conducted in a manner unusually harmful to the individual. See, e. g., *Tennessee* v. *Garner,* 471 U. S. 1. The making of a traffic stop out of uniform does not remotely qualify as such an extreme practice. pp. 816-819.

53 F.3d 371, affirmed.

SCALIA, J., delivered the opinion for a unanimous Court.

Lisa Burget Wright argued the cause for petitioners.

With her on the briefs were A. J. Kramer, Neil H. Jaffee, and G. Allen Dale.

James A. Feldman argued the cause for the United States.

On the brief were Solicitor General Days, Acting Assistant Attorney General Keeney, Deputy Solicitor General Dreeben, and Paul A. Engelmayer. *

*Briefs of *amici curiae* urging reversal were filed for the American Civil Liberties Union by *Steven R. Shapiro* and *Susan N. Herman;* and for the National Association of Criminal Defense Lawyers by *Natman Schaye* and *Walter B. Nash III.*

Briefs of *amici curiae* urging affirmance were filed for the Criminal Justice Legal Foundation by *Kent S. Scheidegger* and *Charles L. Hobson;* and for the State of California et al. by *Daniel E. Lungren,* Attorney General of California, *George Williamson,* Chief Assistant Attorney General, *Ronald A. Bass,* Senior Assistant Attorney General, *Joan Killeen* and *Catherine A. Rivlin,* Supervising Deputy Attorneys General, and *Christina V. Kuo,* Deputy Attorney General; and by the Attorneys General for their respective States as follows: *M. Jane Brady* of Delaware,

Maryland v. Wilson - 519 U.S. 408, 117 S. CT. 882 (1997)[5]

RULE:

An officer making a traffic stop may order passengers to get out of the car pending completion of the stop.

FACTS:

A Maryland state trooper saw a car driving in excess of the posted speed limit. The trooper

---

[5] https://www.lexisnexis.com/community/casebrief/p/casebrief-maryland-v-wilson-487810325

observed that (1) the car had no regular license tag, and (2) a torn piece of paper bearing the name of a car rental agency dangled from the rear of the car. The trooper activated his car's lights and sirens and signaled for the car to pull over. In the course of his pursuit of the car for a mile and a half before it finally pulled over, the trooper noticed that two passengers in the car turned to look at him several times, ducked below sight level, and then reappeared. After the car pulled over and the trooper approached the car on foot, the driver alighted and met the trooper halfway. The driver produced a valid driver's license, and the trooper instructed the driver to return to the car and retrieve the car rental documents. During his encounter with the driver, the trooper had noticed that the car's front-seat passenger was sweating and appeared extremely nervous. While the driver was sitting in the driver's seat looking for the rental documents, the trooper ordered the front-seat passenger out of the car. When the passenger did so, a quantity of crack cocaine fell to the ground. The passenger was then arrested and charged with possession of cocaine with intent to distribute. Before trial in the Circuit Court for Baltimore County, Maryland, the accused moved to suppress the evidence on the ground that the trooper's ordering him out of the car constituted an unreasonable seizure. The circuit court granted the accused's motion to suppress. On appeal, the Court of Special Appeals of Maryland affirmed, expressing the view that the rule that a police officer may as a matter of course order the driver of a lawfully stopped car to exit the vehicle did not apply to passengers. The Court of Appeals of Maryland denied certiorari.

ISSUE:

May a police officer order a passenger form a lawfully stopped car to exit the vehicle?

ANSWER:

Yes.

CONCLUSION:

On certiorari, the Supreme Court of the United States held that consistent with the Fourth Amendment, a police officer making a traffic stop may order passengers to get out of the car pending completion of the stop after applying a test that balanced the public interest and the individual's right to personal security free from arbitrary interference by law officers. Thus, it reversed the lower court's judgment and remanded the case for further proceedings consistent with the Court's opinion.

Commonwealth v. Clayborne, 2021 WL 4487288 (Ken. 2021)[6]

The United States Supreme Court has held that officers may not extend or prolong traffic stops without reasonable, articulable suspicion to conduct further criminal investigation. (*Rodriguez v. United States*, 575 U.S. 348 (2015): A stop may "last no longer than is necessary to effectuate the initial purpose of the stop…Authority for the seizure thus ends when tasks tied to the traffic infraction are—or reasonably should have been—completed." A traffic detention must last no longer than necessary to resolve the suspected traffic violation, either by warning, citation or hearing an explanation from the driver. The detention and

---

[6] https://www.lexipol.com/resources/blog/paint-by-the-numbers-in-traffic-stops/

investigation must be reasonably related to the initial reason for the stop, unless other factors support additional reasonable suspicion (*United States v. Hill*, 852 F.3d 377 (4th Cir. 2017); *United States v. Gil*, 204 F.3d 1347 (11th Cir.), *cert. denied*, 531 U.S. 951 (2000)). Any further detention must be supported by reasonable suspicion of more serious criminal activity. Most courts rigidly apply the *Rodriguez* rule, and that's what happened in this case. An officer stopped Ikia Clayborne after a computer check showed a record for a suspended license and a "verify for proof of insurance" associated with the vehicle's owner. The officer found the driver had a suspended license, and that both the driver and passenger (Clayborne) had records of drug crimes. The officer then requested for a drug detector dog team to come to the scene.

The dog team arrived 10 minutes later, at which point the officer had not yet completed the traffic citation. When the dog team arrived, he quit writing the citation, exited his vehicle and briefed the drug dog detector handler on why he called for a dog. The officer then asked the driver and Clayborne to exit the vehicle and explained the dog sniff procedure to them as they stood by the patrol car. The dog gave a positive response near the passenger door and an officer found a bag of cocaine on the ground underneath the door.

U.S. Supreme Court

Chimel v. California, 395 U.S. 752 (1969)

Chimel v. California

No. 770

Argued March 27, 1969

Decided June 23, 1969

395 U.S. 752

Syllabus

Police officers, armed with an arrest warrant but not a search warrant, were admitted to petitioner's home by his wife, where they awaited petitioner's arrival. When he entered, he was served with the warrant. Although he denied the officers' request to "look around," they conducted a search of the entire house "on the basis of the lawful arrest." At

[7]petitioner's trial on burglary charges, items taken from his home were admitted over objection that they had been unconstitutionally seized. His conviction was affirmed by the California appellate courts, which held, despite their acceptance of petitioner's contention that the arrest warrant was invalid, that, since the arresting officers had procured the warrant "in good faith," and since, in any event, they had had sufficient information to constitute probable cause for the arrest, the arrest was lawful. The courts also held that the search was justified as incident to a valid arrest.

Held: Assuming the arrest was valid, the warrantless search of petitioner's house cannot

---

[7] https://supreme.justia.com/cases/federal/us/395/752/

be constitutionally justified as incident to that arrest. Pp. 395 U. S. 755-768.

(a) An arresting officer may search the arrestee's person to discover and remove weapons and to seize evidence to prevent its concealment or destruction, and may search the area "within the immediate control" of the person arrested, meaning the area from which he might gain possession of a weapon or destructible evidence. Pp. 395 U. S. 762-763.

(b) For the routine search of rooms other than that in which an arrest occurs, or for searching desk drawers or other closed or concealed areas in that room itself, absent well recognized exceptions, a search warrant is required. P. 395 U. S. 763.

(c) While the reasonableness of a search incident to arrest depends upon "the facts and circumstances -- the total atmosphere of the case," those facts and circumstances must be viewed in the light of established Fourth Amendment principles, and the only reasoned distinction is one between (1) a search of the person arrested and the area within his reach, and (2) more extensive searches. Pp. 395 U. S. 765-766.

(d) *United Ste v. Rabinowitz,* 339 U. S. 56, and *Harris v. United States,* 331 U. S. 145, on their facts, and insofar as the principles they stand for are inconsistent with this decision, are no longer to be followed. P. 395 U. S. 768.

(e) The scope of the search here was unreasonable under the Fourth and Fourteenth Amendments, as it went beyond petitioner's person and the area from within which he might have obtained a weapon or something that could have been used as evidence against him, and there was no constitutional justification, in the absence of a search warrant, for extending the search beyond that area. P. 395 U. S. 768.

Contempt of Cop

One of the biggest causes of sustained complaints on a traffic stop is "Contempt of Cop". We've all seen it once or twice in our career or you will see it. From a former supervisor's perspective, I'm here to help you navigate through it.

More now than every person on a traffic stop is filming you. Either from within the car or a "bystander" outside the vehicle. You need to assume that every traffic stop is recorded and the video can and will be scrutinized at a later time.

If you approach a traffic stop with the same attitude, report, and methodical questions or requests, this should not concern you. Where we as a profession fall into a trap is when you have no structure, or don't seek out the proper skill sets like Dave and Mike provide in this book is where you will find yourself in Internal Affairs.

A smart and articulate officer or deputy can see someone baiting them from a mile away. You need to navigate through those obstacles. You need to adapt and be innovative. The days of spitting off case law to a driver and saying, "Look it up later" are over. YOU need to keep printed copies of the case law with you and hand them to the driver. Think that's stupid? Think about it for a second. You've provided documented proof of your authority to do X. If they refuse to accept the documentation, document in your report the efforts you made and the refusal to accept the documentation you went the extra mile to provide. Think about how that looks on body camera footage or the drivers/violators video.

If they accept the documentation have them read it sitting on the curb. This is an excellent way to keep them occupied and focused on the paperwork and not with arguing with you or obstructing a search. Still, think it's stupid? Think about going into court for a suppression hearing or for trial and the judge or jury hears that you provide case law to EVERY driver/violator in an effort to "educate" them. Does that sound like a half-assed cop? Sounds to me like a dedicated, organized, and methodical officer.

As a former supervisor that's conducted countless internal investigations on traffic stop complaints one of the main things I looked at was the officer's ability to de-escalate or defuse the situation. Did the officer amp the complainant up? Did the officer throw in a couple of violations because the driver/passenger was being an asshole?

More times than not this would happen and it would really limit what I could do for my officers. If you see that the situation is getting worse or that this person is clearly having an issue with you, what de-escalating measures are you utilizing? The act of not doing anything is worse than the original complaint.

Utilize de-escalation tactics to limit your exposure to complaints and being derailed from the traffic stop. Sometimes it pays to bring in the "mother figure" or "father figure" while you toss a vehicle. You'd be surprised how much that person can be an advantage to gathering intel. I've done it as a supervisor on the scene. While my officers are searching a vehicle, the violator gives a tremendous amount of information. Where they came from? Who they were with? Use de-escalation to your advantage!

Lastly, don't force an investigation for the sake of sticking it to someone grinding your gears. If it's not a case, don't make it a case. Is the juice worth the squeeze? Only you can answer that, don't allow your backup to encourage you to push a case that's not ripe. Walking away is not defeat. That's a tough thing for us in this profession, walking away… I've seen it a lot, officers are fixated on "the big case" and sacrifice years of training, case law, and common sense to make a case just to have it tossed out in court. Don't be that person.

The Fire is Lit

It started with, "Good afternoon sir, Patrolman Mike Tamez, Kingsville Police, can I please see your driver's license and proof of insurance?" With documents in hand, I asked the driver to exit his vehicle. As the driver took his first step back towards his in-tow 2002 Chevrolet Blazer, I never imagined this would also be my first step down the road of Criminal Interdiction. In 2003 we were in the midst of beginning a new highway interdiction initiative, "Operation Stone Garden." Shortly after 9/11 the federal government began an overtime grant designed to proactively hunt down terrorists traveling on interstates and highways, Stone Garden was now the fuel for that chase. Prior to that day, I had attended law enforcement training focused on "interdiction;" however, still did not have the intimate training necessary for the correct application. In the industry of interdicting criminals, training was not what it is today, convenient and available, so we relied heavily on OJT (on-the-job training). Yes, I understood criminal interdiction and its goal but the actual application and interdicting was so foreign because hands-on training from experts in the field was absent. Nonetheless, I tried, and today that hands-on trial would finally see results. I knew enough to ask questions relating to the driver's trip but not enough to understand the true meaning of his responses. One thing was certain since experience in behavior analysis was absent, subjective questioning was the route I chose. Where are you coming from and where are you going, I asked. North Carolina and McAllen were his answers. Nothing suspicious there except a long trip to drop off a car I believed could have been purchased somewhere in the Rio Grande Valley. Why the long trip with an in-tow Blazer? In-tow meaning the Blazer was being towed by another vehicle. Oh, just taking it for a friend because he bought it in North Carolina and needed it transported down here. Hope the ends justify the means, I thought. At that time my only standard for passing the, should I search, judgment was old, would I be willing to do that question. Of course not, so why would he? Remembering I did not see luggage as I scanned both vehicles walking up during my initial approach, I asked, how many days are you staying down here? Only two days and I'm going back. Weird I thought because nobody would stay somewhere for two days and not take a change of clothes or hygiene. Knowing none of this was illegal but (according to my frame of reference) was uncommon, I believed there was a need to search both vehicles. Eventually, I asked for and was granted consent to search both vehicles. As I had approached every search prior to that day, I checked natural cavities within both vehicles hoping to find the elusive cash load I've heard about others finding along this same stretch of highway. Eventually, I was joined by another officer, Gus Ruiz from the Kleberg County Sheriff's Office, who must have seen my futile attempt at what I considered a thorough search. Gus was a seasoned officer with years of successful interdiction experiences and a world of knowledge I would eventually take advantage of during hands-on vehicle searches later in my career. I searched the first vehicle while Gus searched the in-tow Blazer. Without warning, I heard the two words I've wanted to hear since becoming an officer interested in criminal interdiction, "Cuff him." I turned to find the source of those prized words and saw Gus laying underneath the Blazer. After cuffing the driver, I returned to Gus and was shown the very first after-factory compartment located during one of my traffic stops. Gus located a false floor built underneath the Blazer's rear cargo factory floor.

Eventually, we would find the compartment's access, which was located underneath the Blazer's rear cargo seats; however, due to not being able to successfully figure out an electronic sequence to properly close a circuit, we were unable to open the access without the help of our dear friend, the Hooligan tool. Yes, we used a tool commonly utilized by breachers to pry outward opening doors to open this electronically sealed compartment door. After several long minutes of slamming the Hooligan's curved fork teeth into a seam, we were able to lift the access door and expose the contraband inside. I'll never forget the anticipation of seeing the fruits of our labored attempts to open the door, it almost felt like the night before Christmas. So, what was inside my first after factory compartment? Although the journey to get to that point was exciting, the thrill was quickly removed when I discovered only one bundle of cash concealed within the false floor. Now, don't mistake my disappointment for displeasure, the small amount of cash (only $50,000) was nowhere near as significant as the education I gained that day.

On that day in Kingsville, Texas I began a journey that would eventually define my entire professional career. This chapter will highlight the optic of experiences, education, and never-ending hunger for self-betterment.

The Criminal Interdiction Mindset

At 720 Interdiction Strategies LLC, we define Criminal interdiction as a proactive policing strategy that marries an officer's experiences and training, to identify criminal activities that have occurred, are in the process of occurring, or will occur in the future. Nowhere in the definition is a criminal act named because the unraveling your skills produce, may result in the discovery of contraband like drugs; the recovery of a kidnapped child; or even the apprehension of a murderer.

Now, there are many definitions for criminal interdiction; however, they each share several commonalities. Proactiveness, training, and some experience are common traits necessary for the success of encountering or uncovering criminal activity. With the right encouragement from fellow officers or an incentive fueled by professional or personal life experiences, you will find the daily motivation to hunt crime before it reaches its victim and produces causalities. Unfortunately, not every officer subscribes to this mentality. Some officers are satisfied with taking calls, working accidents, and writing tickets; however, never cast doubt on their willingness to step up when the job requires the fearlessness necessary for response to a priority 1 call for service. Not everyone will share your drive, and some may question your tactics; however, what you produce with righteous police work will eventually drown out the disparagement from others. Notice, I said, "righteous police work." Not questionable, not unethical, not immoral, and especially not illegal. Everything you must do and every decision you make must be beyond reproach and with an extreme sense of righteousness. I'm not saying most officers operate outside the walls of righteousness, I'm simply stating there's a misguided assumption that criminal interdiction officers walk the line of committing civil rights violations, namely the 4th Amendment to the United States Constitution. Exploring and gaining a deep understanding of your state's laws should be the priority of every law enforcement officer because there's always a possibility of surfacing criminal acts. This deep understanding of your legal limitations should be the absolute foundation upon which the pillars of your criminal interdiction mindset are built. Once you have solidified the legal knowledge base, you're well on the way to forming a strategy to uncover hidden crimes.

"Criminal interdiction officer" is not necessarily a title, it's a mindset. When you're told, "Go beyond the ticket," this usually infers to look beyond the face value of a traffic stop or encounter because what's lurking beyond may be far more dubious than a traffic violation. Fortunately, some agencies have created teams whose sole assignment is to conduct proactive or directed patrol law enforcement duties in order to discover crimes or bring to light the likelihood of a future criminal act that may occur. Unlike reactive police strategies, your mission is to initiate the discovery of the crime. Whether in a full or part-time criminal interdiction capacity, your strategy never changes because your mindset should always remain the same. Contrary to popular belief within the law enforcement profession, criminal interdiction is not solely associated with stopping vehicles on major United States Highways or Interstates. Although the contraband and roadway may differ, the tactics remain effective because success with committing the crime relies on the criminal's ability to deceive.

Fortunately, this book centers around one component of policing, the traffic stop. As you read this section, consider using the same tactics and analytical mindset as you perform day-to-day duties within your agency. Although the principles and strategies discussed in this section will center around traffic stops, their applications have far-reaching use. Just remember this, criminals only succeed when they've managed to deceive you. As you'll learn in this section, your ultimate success in criminal interdiction lies with your ability to properly evaluate behavior away from a baseline as it pertains to emotionally relevant stimuli. We will remove the myths and subjectiveness commonly associated with criminal interdiction, so you can move forward with success on the roadside and in the

courtroom.

The Much-Needed Shift

Several years ago, my wife, Rebecca, and I were traveling from Corpus Christi, Texas to a small rural city in north Texas, Kemp. Since getting married, Rebecca and I had yet to visit her "Nee-Nee," so this was my inaugural visit. Unfortunately, neither of us knew how to get from Corpus Christi to Kemp, so we relied on Google Maps to guide our journey. As we neared, Google Maps diverted us to a farm-to-market road which would eventually lead us directly into the city. Like most road trips, Rebecca and I spent the time laughing, talking, and listening to the radio. Unfortunately, I was deep in conversation with Rebecca when I glanced at the rear-view mirror and saw a law enforcement patrol unit behind our newly purchased Denali

Tahoe. I immediately looked down at the speedometer and noticed I was over the speed limit; unfortunately, my fate was already sealed. I watched as the patrol unit's overhead red and blue emergency lights activated, signaling the beginning of a traffic stop.

As expected from any motorist I encounter during a traffic stop, I pulled off the roadway and stopped in a safe location. Eventually, the officer made his way to the window and in a very professional manner requested my driver's license and vehicle insurance. With documents in hand, the officer asked me to exit and move to the rear of our Tahoe. Let me preface the rest of this story with, I never told the officer I was a Criminal Interdiction Agent with the South Texas

Specialized Crimes and Narcotics Task Force, a team with a storied reputation within the interdiction community. Nonetheless, my law enforcement career would hold zero bearing on the outcome of this traffic stop because I would never attempt to influence the officer's decision by telling him I too was an officer.

    Once at the rear of our vehicle, the officer explained my violation and asked why I was speeding. Instead of making up a bullshit excuse, I simply said, "No sir, was just involved in a conversation with my wife and wasn't paying attention." Eventually, the topic of our trip became the subject of the officer's questions. I was asked where we were coming from, where were we going, and what was the reason for our trip. Simple enough, I told the officer we were coming from Corpus Christi and were traveling to visit my wife's grandmother in Kemp. Without hesitation, the officer responded, "Kemp, you know you're on the wrong highway if you're going to Kemp?" My inner voice immediately said, "this guy's about to try and interdict me." This obviously wasn't the time to play games and try tripping up the officer, so I told him the truth, "No I didn't know that I'm using a Garmin for navigation, so I followed her directions." Something must have aroused this young officer's suspicion because his tone changed as he asked questions regarding the specifics of our trip. Even after I told the officer that Google was our guide, something he could have easily asked to see, he continued telling me that we were on the wrong road and if we were going to Kemp, we should be on a different road. After a short exchange of question and answer, the officer left me and went to question Rebecca, who was still seated in the Tahoe.

I awaited the officer's return, which eventually came approximately 5-minutes later. Somewhat calmer, the officer asked if I was in possession of a weapon and if I was a law enforcement officer; I answered, "yes" to each. Immediately the officer fired back, "Why didn't you tell me?" Seeing the opening, I immediately knew this was an opportunity to teach a very valuable lesson that could one day help this young officer. I responded with, "Does me being a cop matter, cops commit crime also."

After several minutes of talking about concealment trends, I was released with only a warning. Guess that day, we both learned valuable lessons. Hopefully, the officer left with a newly discovered mindset of non-biased decision-making because I certainly learned the lesson that training must evolve.

As we began driving away, Rebecca and I started to debrief the encounter. Rebecca was asked the same questions I was however, she was also asked for consent to search our vehicle. When asked about weapons in our vehicle, Rebecca told the officer we had several pistols and one 40mm grenade launcher. Yes, a grenade launcher. Fortunately, Rebecca worked for Safariland, so our second goal for the trip was to deliver the grenade launcher to members of the Dallas Police Department's SWAT team. Eventually Rebecca's responses about guns segwayed into my status as a criminal interdiction officer for the South Texas Specialized Crimes and Narcotics Task Force.

After learning about the officer's request to search, I began replaying the encounter in my head. What became an overwhelming theory was why the officer wanted to search our vehicle even though we never lied to him. It hit me, we were in possession of almost every "indicator of criminal activity" taught to most curious and proactive officers throughout the country. Marine Corps support stickers on the Tahoe's cargo hatch window represented, "good guy stickers." Our total of 3 cell phones was seen as "burner phones." Our vehicle was a higher-end Tahoe model, which was understood as a trophy for being successful smugglers. Only one key was seated inside the Tahoe's ignition because the vehicle truly wasn't ours and belonged to a smuggling organization. Unfortunately, the officer was grossly mistaken on this one. Every single item the officer viewed as an "indicator of criminal activity" was easily explainable had he asked. Stopping us and wanting to search our vehicle did one thing for that officer, it wasted his time if indeed his goal was to catch us smuggling drugs.

Although there wasn't an opportunity to question the young officer and challenge my theory about his decision to ask for consent to search, fate would soon bring us together. Approximately two years later while working United States Highway 77 in Kleberg County, Texas, I saw an officer searching a truck all by himself. Never a supporter of searching alone, I stopped to help the officer. As I approached the officer his identity was immediately apparent, he was the same officer that stopped Rebecca and I on our way to Nee-Nee's. After a short reunion, the officer asked if I could speak with the truck's driver and passenger because they only spoke Spanish. Immediately my inner dialogue wondered why the officer was searching this truck if his ability to ask and interpret responses was greatly hindered by the language barrier. Nonetheless, I spoke with the truck's occupants and came to one certain conclusion, they were not lying.

Following my conversation with the truck's occupants, I met with the officer and shared my opinion. Just as I thought, my view fell on deaf ears. When asked for a reason to continue searching, the officer said, "Well they have a Ferrari sticker." Just like that, my theory was confirmed. Instead of searching the truck based on a mountain of reasonable suspicion, the officer's decision progressed because he saw one sticker that had been associated with drug trafficking organizations in the past.

Reflecting on both encounters with the officer coupled with a little deductive reasoning, I knew the foundation of his reasonable suspicion was solely built on a mindset of subjectiveness. Knowing how misleading this style of policing was, I decided to do my part and teach officers what I have been taught and continue to learn throughout my 22 years as a law enforcement officer. My commitment to helping officers came in the form of 720 Interdiction Strategies LLC, a company built to bridge the gap between training and reality. Although I knew it wouldn't be easy, quietly my goal was to eliminate the antiquated tactics taught in cookie-cutter training events. Instead of teaching officers to look for "items of interest," I would use my body camera footage to demonstrate the effectiveness of observing and listening. Smuggling trends may come and go; however, as long as officers are stopping cars, the possibility of unraveling criminal activity rests solely on our ability to communicate and decipher deviations in behavior. Regardless of where an officer works, there will always be one commonality that can lead you to discover something much more nefarious than a traffic violation; that singular commonality is communication.

Single key, multiple air fresheners, no luggage, too much luggage, not enough luggage, more-than-one cell phone, 3rd party rental, renter paid cash for the rental car, smuggler saints in the car, and of course, good guy stickers. If you've attended criminal interdiction training, chances are you've heard an instructor classify each of those as "Items of interest" or clues commonly associated with drug smugglers. Unfortunately, these are the same cookie-cutter "indicators" I was taught when attending my first criminal interdiction class almost 20 years ago. Almost like a checklist, instructors would stock the young unexperienced officer's interdiction toolbox with subjective clues that were sure to be encountered if indeed a person was in the process of, was about to be or had already been smuggling drugs, money or weapons. An instructor would qualify each item with a short personal story of their encounter with a "cartel smuggler" possessing some if not all those items. Commonly the report narrative would include language to the effect of, "I observed a single key in the ignition." Unfortunately to the untrained ordinary juror, this alone will mean absolutely nothing without a statement justifying the importance of that single key and its significance to support the officer's conclusions. So, immediately following the observation statement, an officer would say something like, "I know from training and experience that smugglers commonly travel with only one key because load vehicles are commonly picked up at the random location (by the smuggler) once contraband has been concealed within it." Ah, there's the ever-so-important nexus. Remember, all this from an observation of a single key in the ignition.

Just how powerful are these "indicators?" Powerful enough to persuade an officer into believing that every motorist traveling with a single key may possibly be a cartel smuggler. Human beings naturally default to truth; however, something clicks the day you take an oath and begin a career in law enforcement. Instead of believing people are inherently good, experience forces us down a pathway of pessimism and cynicism. So instead of viewing a single key through the optic of innocence, daily experiences with criminals reinforced with flawed training cause an officer to subjectively believe criminal activity may be afoot. Regrettably, these indicator-based beliefs are compounded as additional "items of interest" are stacked even before a traffic stop is made. If an officer sees pro-police stickers on the back of a vehicle, they're no longer a show of appreciation and support, instead, they're an item of interest meant to portray the driver as a good guy when indeed he's a criminal. Rosaries are no longer a display of faith; they are now meant to protect a criminal from law enforcement. There's no question many of these items have been present during many encounters with criminals; however, the vast majority of people possessing them are doing so with innocence and free from any nefarious intention. What this fatal flaw in law enforcement training has done is create an officer that bases his judgment on what a person displays in a vehicle more so than the content within their conversation. What we have done is widen our goal of finding a true needle in the haystack.

So, why the need for a paradigm shift? Simply put, this training model builds a conclusion from a foundation of subjectiveness. If an officer's decision to search a car is solely based on these learned indicators of criminal activity, the majority of vehicles searched will result in little-to-no contraband being found. Why? Because every item identified as an "Item of interest" can be possessed by any innocent motorist. Now I'll concede that many of those items may be found in vehicles transporting contraband, but I recommend meeting several criteria before being used as Reasonable Articulable Suspicion (RAS).

1) Have a deep understanding of the item's significance and its nexus to criminal activity. This understanding will solidify your ability to tie the items into the development of RAS contextually as it's applied to your current traffic stop. In other words, does the item of interest share the same value with every traffic stop or does it have independent value to your current

stop. Simply put, the item should not be so broad that it's labeled an "item of interest" with every single stop because the totality of circumstances must include verbal/non-verbal communication.

2) Properly articulate each and every item of interest individually. Although the totality will eventually develop from the combination of each item of interest, you must leave zero doubt in the mind of a judge or juror that even alone, they are powerful enough to arouse suspicion.

3) Have training to support your decision to qualify a specific item as an "item of interest." We work in a profession that values validation through education. During any judicial testimony, officers are given an opportunity to qualify their

experiences for the judge and jury because it speaks to credibility. Without education to support your claim, you will be defenseless against an aggressive attorney attempting to impeach your credibility.

Unfortunately, many in the criminal interdiction training industry have fallen into the cookie-cutter training loop. Instead of officers teaching officers from professional experiences, they gravitate to a vicious cycle of regurgitating flaws taught by others. Speaking from many professional experiences, many of these "items of interest" were prominent with many Transnational Drug Trafficking Organizations (TDTO's). It was common to catch a smuggler with a single key, good-guy stickers, multiple air fresheners, several cell phones, and narco-saint figurines as they transported contraband from source city to source city. Notice I said, "were prominent." In 2011 I stopped a gentleman by the name of Pena-Gonzales on U.S. Highway 77 in Kleberg County, Texas. Prior to the stop, I observed 4 law enforcement support stickers plastered on the vehicle's rear cargo door, 7 air fresheners in plain view strung throughout the passenger compartment, and several rosaries hanging from the rearview mirror. During the course of my interview with the driver, I also heard many deceptive clues and observed many signs of physical nervousness. Eventually, I asked for and was given verbal consent to search Pena-Gonzalez's vehicle, which eventually led me to the discovery of nearly $700,000. Fast forward to the eventual 5th Circuit Court of Appeals decision, this case established the use of these items as accepted reasonable suspicion. So, if we won and created case law, why the need for a shift?

In order to be successful, TDTO smugglers must transport contraband from city to city without being interdicted; therefore, they adjust the Tactics Techniques and Procedures (TTPs) accordingly. Pena-Gonzalez made national news and gave an open-source insight into what interdiction officers look for during the entire course of a traffic stop. With the education gained from the Pena-Gonzalez case, many smugglers hit the road without items that could suggest a crime was in progress. So, what! Take away every subjective "item of interest" and still we will win. If there's a consequence, like being caught smuggling contraband, introducing a stimulus like your police car, uniform, or emotionally relevant questions will almost guarantee a successful outcome for law enforcement.

Double-edged Biology

This is not your typical hunter's hide because the hunt is not your typical hunt. Unlike the game harvested on a ranch, mountain range, or lease, your trophy is smart, feels emotion, knows right from wrong, and is biologically gifted with elusiveness when confronted. Those attributes alone can create a sense of pessimism for a successful outcome to any interdiction stop; however, they are also the crux of what you will use to interdict the right vehicle, evaluate the relevant behaviors, and build a case that can withstand scrutiny from defense attorneys. In other words, human biology is a fucked double edge sword.

Like our ancestors avoiding saber-toothed tigers, modern humans react instinctively and in real-time to the modern threats around them. Our eyes are constantly scanning in search of harmful situations because we know, if we're to stay safe, we must avoid the source of that very uncomfortable feeling within. Once identified, the stimulus of your fear immediately invokes a reaction from the limbic part of your brain. Your non-cognitive response comes from a history of learning about harmful situations, not necessarily experiencing them. Your brain soaks in those memories and creates a plan of action in the event it, unfortunately, crosses paths with something similar. Stored in the subconscious, the fear-based emotional responses, sometimes referred to as heuristics or somatic markers, provoke the sympathetic nervous system. Your body's non-cognitive emotional response has officially begun.

Picture this, you're operating a complete stranger's vehicle, in transit from one major city to another. What you're doing is not a favor, it's a job. Currency is nothing but payment for goods or services. Unfortunately for you, the currency you're transporting is the proceeds from drug sales and the service you're providing is transportation for a ruthless drug trafficking organization. As you crest an overpass, a marked law enforcement patrol unit comes into view. Immediately you realize the potential of being stopped and every negative emotion you will experience if your criminal act is uncovered. Realizing the possibility, you instantly classify that patrol unit as a threat. Now your Limbic brain is in survival mode. In an effort to keep you alive, your limbic brain releases adrenaline to kickstart the sympathetic nervous system. Without thought, your foot comes off the gas causing a decrease in speed because you must eliminate any conceivable reason to be stopped. As you approach the patrol unit, you notice an increase in your heartbeat and a strengthening of your appendages. Why? Because blood is being rushed to your arms and legs so you can fight harder, run faster, jump higher. Knowing your fast approaching the stimulus of this non-cognitive physiological response, your limbic brain desires a relief from the anxiety and stress; therefore, you either attempt to change lanes and create distance between you and the source of your anxiety or you turn away right as you cross the patrol unit's front bumper. Not only did you turn away from the patrol unit to avoid any visual contact with your threat, but you also began stroking your hair. Believe it or not, this reaction is also associated with the Limbic brain. What may be perceived as an innocent touching of the hair, is also known as a pacifying movement because there was an external stimulus that prompted it. This pacifying movement serves one goal, to relieve the body of energy caused by the adrenaline dump.

Now you're past the unit, stress alleviated right? Wrong! Knowing the patrol unit can leave the median and pull you over, your brain and sympathetic nervous system are still in survival mode. As long as there's a line of sight between you and the patrol unit, there's a need to keep a watchful eye because that once stationary threat can quickly become mobile.

Unfortunately for you, the officer occupying that stationary patrol car is trained to look for those limbic-based responses, so he leaves the median with one goal in mind, have a conversation with you. As the patrol unit closes the distance with your vehicle, your sympathetic nervous system is in a state of absolute panic. Now you realize the possibility of coming face to face with the source of your physiological changes. As you see the patrol unit's red and blue emergency lights activate, there's a quick rehearsal of the story created before you even began this trip. "If I'm pulled over, I'll say that I'm coming from the house and am on the way to visit an aunt because I haven't seen her in a while." Perfect, a reasonable story that explains the reason for your trip. Well, perfect unless the officer pulling you over has been trained properly to identify deviations in behavior.

Once stopped, you're preparing for the encounter that can only end in two ways; one, you're released or two, you're going to jail. What you don't know is, regardless of all the preparations you've made, this attempt to smuggle drugs is minutes away from coming to an end. Why? Because this officer understands two things: 1) your limbic responses relay truthful emotion and 2) no matter how many times you've rehearsed the fictional cover story, the events never happened, so with a few questions, he will uncover your plot. So, although biology has provided one hell of a system to ensure survival, it has also made behaviors obvious to someone with the knowledge that can interpret their true meanings. Thus, biology truly is a double-edged sword.

How to win

"If you want to win the judge and jury, you must show a comparison."

Mike Tamez

There's only one thing a criminal must do to be successful. Regardless of the crime, they must lie. Smuggling drugs, committing murder, stealing a bag of candy from the convenience store when confronted by law enforcement, they must lie to avoid detention, arrest, and prosecution. Therefore, a successful outcome hinges on your ability to articulate human behavior as it pertains to the strategic stimulus you will provide. Since the overall theme of this book focuses on traffic stops, your stimulus must come in the form of formulated questions that will emotionally activate the limbic brain. Why is this so important? Since the limbic brain is responsible for keeping you alive with non-cognitive emotional responses, we consider that split-second response truthful. If you're an officer focused on intercepting drugs, cash, or weapons smuggled from one source city to another, we have developed six key topics that hold great emotional relevance as it pertains to this specific criminal activity.

Those 6 key topics of emotional relevance are:

    1) Origin. "Where are you coming from?"

    2) Destination. "Where are you going?"

    3) Purpose. "Why are you going there?"

    4) Time. "How many days will you be there?"

    5) Relationship. "Who's with you?" "Who were you visiting?"

6) Contraband. "Are you traveling with anything illegal hidden inside the car?"

In a nutshell, these specific emotionally relevant questions are carefully chosen because of their association with in-transit criminal activity. If the driver is involved in smuggling, he must lie about all or some of those topics because the truth will only lead to the discovery of a criminal act.

Consider this, you pull a vehicle over for a traffic violation. After greeting the driver and identifying yourself, you explain the violation and begin the process of issuing a written warning. While filling out the warning you begin to ask the driver those 6 emotionally relevant questions (in no order). As you come to the question of purpose, you ask the driver, "So, what did you do in New Jersey?" If the truth is, the driver was delivering a large amount of cocaine, he must respond with an answer that cannot associate him with criminal activity or arouse suspicion. Within a split-second of you asking the question, the driver's brain recalls the truth of what he did in New Jersey. Knowing he cannot be true because his freedom will be jeopardized, his limbic brain is immediately activated to deal with the dangerous situation. As his chest begins to visibly rise and fall, you see his right-hand move to the top of his head as he begins playing with his hair. Ah-ha, the sympathetic nervous system is now in survival mode. Instead of answering your question, the driver responds with, "Huh?" Knowing this is a common technique used to create think space, you do not repeat the question. Instead, you stare at the driver and await his answer. After a 2-second pause, the driver answers, "Oh, I was visiting my sick aunt, I had not seen her in about a year." Recognizing the limbic response, you believe the driver perceived danger with the content of your question. Since the driver answered your question without ever having it repeated, you realize there may be an underlying explanation that must be discovered. Now you know, there's much more work to be done if you're to elicit what truly occurred while in New Jersey.

Defense attorney: "Officer, you said my client had a deviation of physical and verbal behavior when you asked about the purpose of their trip; how do you not know that's not his normal behavior?"

Believe it or not, this is a wonderful question because it's certainly a thought-provoking theory for the judge and jury to consider. Anticipation is what sets the standard for everything we do in law enforcement. In this case, anticipating this theory teaches us a very profound lesson, know the driver's normal behavior. If we're to recognize distinct changes/

deviations in behavior, we must first establish a known behavioral baseline.

Before we begin to establish the baseline, we must first remove something that will absolutely destroy how you interpret all communication, you're biased. As a practice, store your professional, personal, and confirmation biases in your gun safe at home before leaving to start a patrol shift. An easy way to rationalize the damage a bias can inflict is by believing only young gang members are capable of smuggling drugs. Unfortunately for that rationalization, it's a lie. People commit in-transit crimes to make money and as far as I know, young adults with gang ties and tattoos, are not the only people wanting to make money. No place for a bias in law enforcement because it only helps to create subjective beliefs.

Understand this, a baseline isn't a difficult task that needs to be backed with case law. Luckily for you, practice is something you do every single day. What's the key element of a baseline question? My recommendation is to make the question one that will not place the listener in a position of fabricating a response. An example, "How old are your kids?" Unless the listener kidnapped his children, this is a response that should not require too much cognitive load on the brain. When you ask anyone a question, evaluate four pieces of their response:

1) Tone

    a. Pitch is neutral

    b. Pitch is high

    c. Pitch is low

2) Rate of speech

    a. Did their rate of speech increase?

    b. Did their rate of speech decrease?

3) Did they answer with contextual consistency?

    a. If you asked a closed-ended question (yes or no response), did they respond with an open-ended response that never answered your question.

b. If you asked an open-ended question, did they provide an answer consistent with the context of your question?

4) Think space

   a. How much time did it take to return an answer for a closed-ended question?

   b. How much time did it take to return an answer to an open-ended question?

Once you identify the individual's baseline behaviors, now you're able to build a comparison. As you ask the 6 emotionally relevant questions, evaluate the responses in the same manner you did the baseline questions. What are you looking for? Simple, deviations in physical responses, like limbic stimulated sympathetic processes, and deviations in verbal responses. Now, if you do see dynamic deviations in behavior, we're not saying this individual is lying; however, you should definitely consider digging a little more into the question that caused the shift.

When it comes to articulation for Reasonable Suspicion remember this, your evaluation of the person's behavior is not a comparison against others you've encountered throughout your career. If you're making statements like, "Nobody else acts like this person when asked the same questions," referring to other encounters with the public, you're doing nothing but helping a defense attorney mount a great argumentative defense against your ability to remain objective. Instead, your comparison needs to be made between their response to emotionally irrelevant questions (baseline) versus emotionally relevant questions. Understand, no two people in the world are created identically; therefore, you can expect different physical and verbal responses to emotionally relevant and irrelevant questions. However, if you evaluate those two types of questions while speaking with one individual on the roadside or in an interview room, you will definitely strengthen your belief that Reasonable Suspicion exists.

Just a small piece of advice

Just wanted to close my section with a few tidbits of advice that can definitely help your career in the criminal interdiction field as well as law enforcement as a whole:

1) If you have to cheat to win, you're really losing. Remember, your actions not only affect you, but they also have far-reaching secondary effects in the form of case law that affect us all.

2) Leave your biases at home when you put the uniform on each day. If you're able to store your bias, you will truly open the opportunity to get better results.

3) Have empathy/share something personal about yourself. This is the best way to

humanize your badge. Not only will empathy help you understand the true reason a criminal is committing a crime, but it will also make you so much more approachable. When you're approachable, you will win. Remember this, "Comfort leads to honesty, discomfort leads to dishonesty."

4) Store the ego. Not only will humility help you amongst your peers but will definitely make you more approachable to the individuals you stop and interview.

5) TRAIN TRAIN TRAIN!!! Currently, within the interdiction training industry, there are many credible companies and instructors

that offer a wide range of specialty courses. Take advantage of the many opportunities and approach each with an open mind and a willingness to learn. NEVER limit yourself to only one instructor or company because I promise you can learn from each. "If you value your career, add value to your career."

Attitude is Contagious:

Is yours worth catching?

I think before we start talking about how to be successful at impaired driving enforcement, we need to take a close look at ourselves. Mike and I both come from a Marine Corps service background. (I'll pause while everyone makes crayon comments) One of the Corps mantras is "every Marine is a rifleman". Regardless if you're assigned to a specialized unit such as a Traffic Safety Unit or Criminal Interdiction Unit, you're a law enforcement officer FIRST! My primary job is to change driving behavior in my jurisdiction. Mostly I do this by stopping cars and evaluating motorists. Now, I can't do this by myself. I need coworkers to back me up on stops, sit on tow sheets, perform drug influence evaluations, review reports, and the list goes on and on. Many times I've gone into a patrol district and took calls for service that were pending or I was close to. It's difficult to go into a district and start stopping cars when the district officers are going call to call to call. Be a team player. I tell folks all the time "my star isn't broken".

What motivates you? I think this is something you need to constantly ask yourself in impaired driving enforcement because there's going to come a time when you get frustrated. Early in my career, my motivation was very self-serving. As a young Marine MP, I figured if I made a DUI case, I could sit down and write paperwork rather than stand on a gate all night long in jungle boots.

When I started my civilian career, I just liked saying "one in custody" over the radio and I worked in a target-rich environment. There was a point where it clicked and I thought "maybe if I arrest more impaired drivers, I'll knock on fewer doors and have to deliver death notifications". At no time during your hiring process did someone tell you that was part of our job. They tell you about all the other cool aspects of law enforcement, but they leave that out. I often go to candlelight vigils, memorial services, and use crash survivors in my company training courses…….because it's important to remember its flesh and blood, brothers, and sisters, husbands and wives, sons and daughters……not just statistics.

Iron sharpens iron. It's easier to hone your craft when someone else is pushing you. Find someone in your agency, or your surrounding area to go to training courses with, bounce off ideas, vent to when you get frustrated.

Finally, would you want others to emulate your attitude? We've all worked with the officer who's never happy. I call it "the golden brick syndrome". You know these people. You can give them a golden brick and they'll find a reason to fuss. "It's too heavy. I have to take it all the way to Atlanta to cash it in. When I get there they only give me $20 bills". Now, I'm a realist. We all have bad days or things that upset us. I put a limit on how long I'll be upset about something. Bob got the promotion instead of me: I'll be upset till 0700 tomorrow then let it go.

Target Selection / Slump Busting / How to Find Drunks

When I first started in civilian law enforcement, I was fortunate enough to come out of field training straight into a specialized unit. I spent six months running around in an unmarked car chasing bad guys. One of the greatest gigs I've had. So I transfer back into uniform and I'm ready to make it happen. I literally stopped EVERYTHING that moved. A defective license plate light wasn't safe within 300 feet of me. I would come out 30 minutes prior to the shift, stop cars on the way to roll call, spend as little time at the office as possible, and I was back at it. Eventually, I'd find an impaired driver but I really had no idea what I was looking for. Mostly it was throwing something against the wall and hoping it would stick. My sergeant would sit in the office for the first three hours of the shift, leave the office, stop one car…..maybe two, and make an arrest. I would LOSE MY MIND! I'd look at Sarge "How do you do that?" He smiles and said, "I know what I'm looking for". Hopefully, this chapter helps you.

First, I had to away from the Friday and Saturday only mindset. People don't just drive impaired on the weekends. In the Movie "Glenn Gary, Glenn Ross" there's a phrase "Always Be Closing". I employ the mindset "Always Be Hunting". Going to coffee in the morning, school zone enforcement, on the way home (yeah I said it). If you want to be successful you have to put forth the effort. Second, know what's going on in your area. It doesn't have to be big events, but they help. St. Patrick's Day is huge here. Go online and see what's going on in your community. There's something going on every day of the week. Monday night football, Two Dollar Tuesdays, Hump day specials, thirsty Thursday, obviously Friday and Saturdays, Sunday fun days. Is there a body of water near you? Rivers, lakes, oceans, etc. Water and booze go together…….. And I'm not talking about a mixer.

Violations I stop fall into four categories: speed, lane violations, turning violations, and following too close.

Speed- I'm not stopping eleven and twelve miles over the speed limit (traditionally). I'm looking for cars that are 20 mph over the speed limit or 10 mph under the speed limit. Now we've all heard "speeding isn't an indicator of impaired driving". NHTSA didn't list it in the top 24 violations because many people are stopped for speeding that isn't impaired. If you look at the general indicators for CNS Depressants (alcohol or ETOH) one is "relaxed inhibitions". You know what I'm talking about. This is the "hold my beer", "zero f$%ks given", "YOLO" moment. When someone is hammering past cars at 83mph in a 60 mph zone, at 0240, it becomes an indicator. 10 mph under the speed limit gets me thinking about drugs that slow the internal clock.

Lane Violations- This is really simple. Crossing lane lines or weaving within the lane. One of the big things I'll look at is how a motorist handles a curve. How far into the apex of the curve do they wait till they start turning. A guy I used to teach with would say "as soon as I see one lane violation, I stop them." I tend to wait for multiple violations. I want to weed out the motorist who sneezed and jerked the wheel or looked down at their phone one time.

<u>Turning Violations</u>- the big one I use for turning is "wide radius turn" or when they extend the turn from the inside lane to the outside lane. Start stopping these and you'll find more impaired drivers.

<u>Following Too Close</u>- This is a violation that we don't stop near enough! In session five of the NHTSA DUI/SFST manual, it says impaired vision occurs at .08% BAC. It only makes sense to stop this.

Roadside Interviewing and Reestablishing Rapport Post Arrest

The defendant provides 90 percent of all evidence in an impaired driving case. How we talk matters. If we come off like a super jerk, people are going to shut down. Recently I watched another law enforcement officer contact a motorist and the first words out of the officer's mouth were "why are you speeding on my highway?' Let's take a look at this statement. It's not YOUR highway. You don't own it and it's not named after you. If it is named after you, and you're still alive, that's pretty impressive! This one sentence set the tone and put the motorist on the defensive. If my wife asks "why didn't you take out the trash?" My heart rate increases and I get nervous. We want to set people at ease so we can figure out if they are involved in criminal activity whether it's impaired driving or smuggling. I introduce myself with my first and last name. "My name is Dave Kopenhaver. I'm a deputy with the sheriff's department. The reason I stopped you is I measured your speed with radar at 81 mph in a posted 60 mph zone. Is everything okay?" I stopped using my rank years ago. It puts you on the same level as the motorist and makes you appear friendlier. "Are you okay?" opens the door and gives them a chance to talk.

Now, NHTSA is going to stroke out when I say this: I don't interview people while they're seated in the car as the book says to. I think it's a bad idea to ask questions about drugs and alcohol while they're sitting in the driver's seat. All it takes is for them to throw it in gear and now you have a pursuit with an impaired driver. I interview them at the rear bumper. Now, I started in an environment where we had to Mirandize people prior to administering field tests so I ask a lot of questions.

Where are you coming from?

Where are to going?

How much have you had to drink?

When did you start?

When did you stop?

Without looking at a watch or a clock what time is it?

On a scale from 1-10, one is stone-cold sober, ten falling down drunk, rate your level of impairment.

So we've put all this together and made an impaired driving arrest. We just changed somebody's life forever. Regardless if it's the first or fifteenth time they've been arrested. Rarely do I field test people by myself so after handcuffing the defendant, I usually pass them off to my partner while I inventory the car or do whatever administrative stuff I need to do. This gives me a breather with the defendant because I just became the bad guy. Believe it or not, nobody is running around thinking "boy, I hope Dave Kopenhaver stops and arrests me tonight." So I'll let them curse my name and tell Phillip or whoever what a lousy cop I am.

One of the big things I try to remember is not to chastise or belittle them; "You could have killed six people tonight!" does not help me. It's probably true, but it doesn't get me where I want to be: a voluntary toxicology sample. I try to explain every step of the process to the defendant because most people haven't been in this position and are scared. Scared of the unknown.

Teamwork Makes the

Dream Work

In February 2006, I went to a highway safety conference in Mobile, Alabama. I was in a stage of my career where I was very disgruntled. I especially wasn't happy with attorneys: Prosecution or defense. I felt like defense attorneys were constantly raking me over the coals and prosecutors weren't doing anything to help me. I was fortunate enough to meet my friend Kimberly who's a prosecutor in North Carolina. In the first 10 minutes of speaking to her, I knew she was as passionate about prosecuting DUI cases as I was about making them. We traded business cards and stayed in touch. A couple of months later she was the keynote speaker for a DUI task force dinner I was a part of. She spoke of how local law enforcement took her under their wing and took an interest in her. I think I wrote down every word she said that night and put it to work in South Carolina.

The biggest hurdle between cops and prosecutors is ego. Law enforcement has an enormous amount of power and responsibility thrust upon our shoulders and is expected to make split-second decisions and don't like to be told when we're wrong. Prosecutors go to school for half a century and don't like to be told by a cop with a Ph.D. (public high school diploma) that they're wrong. So how do we close the gap? Easy…… TACOS. Who doesn't like tacos? If you don't I don't trust you. In all seriousness, break some bread with your prosecutor. Find one you can bond with and get the ball rolling. I was fortunate enough to build a relationship quickly with my prosecutor's office here in Columbia.

Karlen and I hit it off from the beginning. Philip and I watched her argue a motion when I first came to the Sheriff's Department. She asked me to review a DUI drugs case for her and our friendship took off. So much that she teaches with us at Integrated Impaired Driving Solutions. I was in the prosecutor's office looking at cases at least once a week. If I wasn't looking at cases, it was sharing a cup of coffee or going to lunch with other prosecutors. Guys in my unit would joke "hey next time you're at the prosecutor's office can you……" You don't have to be math experts to figure out more cases are coming in than can be taken to trial. If they know my name and face, maybe my cases have a better outcome.

www.ingramcontent.com/pod-product-compliance
Lightning Source LLC
Chambersburg PA
CBHW031416210526
45464CB00005B/1918